Birds in the Street

The City Pigeon Book

A STEPPING-STONE BOOK

Birds in the Street

The City Pigeon Book

By

Winifred

and

Cecil Lubell

Parents' Magazine Press • *New York*

Here's a pigeon
on the street—
stiff legs,
walking like a wound-up toy.

Pink feet
on gray concrete.
Eyes red
Bobbing head—
be-bop, be-bop, be-bop—
in time with its feet.

Be-bop,
then stops
to peck the ground;
then circles round.
Be-bop,
then stops again.
Perhaps a danger signal
reached its brain.
Here comes a car, a bus,
a taxi in a rush.

They'll run it down!
But no—
for just in time
it lifts its wings,
takes off,
is safe,
is flying free.

How beautiful!
A bird in flight!
No stiff legs now,
no pigeon toes,
no bobbing head,
no be-bop walk.

A graceful, winged thing,
an airborne creature
wild against the sky.

The beat of feathers
echoes down the city street
and makes
a country sound.
Nice to have around.

Yes, many people like pigeons. They like to see them flying wild against the sky.

But some people hate pigeons. Oh, how they hate pigeons!

This is what some of them say:

"Pigeons are pests . . . pests . . . pests!"

Other people say:

"Pigeons make an awful mess!"

"They ruin the statues with their droppings."

"They make the buildings filthy and we have to spend thousands of dollars to clean them."

Most of that is true, but buildings and statues have to be cleaned for other reasons, too. It's not just pigeons who make them dirty.

Some people say it's bad to feed pigeons in the city because rats come in to get the food they leave.

Many people can't stand the noise pigeons make. You often hear them say:

"Those pigeons are driving me crazy! They made a nest right over my window and they wake me up at the crack of dawn with their billing and cooing."

And a lot of people believe pigeons are dangerous. They think pigeon droppings carry a disease.

Is that true?

Yes, it is true. But the same thing is true of droppings from chickens and many other animals. When the droppings dry up, they become powdery. Then, if you get the dust up your nose, you might catch the disease.

It's not dangerous in the open air, but it might be dangerous inside empty old buildings where pigeons have made nests and left big piles of droppings.

You should stay away from places like that.

Because of these things many people don't like pigeons.

But there are just as many people who love pigeons.

They say very nice things about pigeons, like this:

"I like to watch the pigeons flying around in front of the library. It's so nice to have a bit of wildlife in the city."

You will also hear them say:

"I like the cooing sound pigeons make. It's very restful."

Pigeon-lovers don't think the birds are dirty. They say:

"People make most of the dirt, not pigeons. Why, pigeons even clean up some of the garbage people throw on the street."

That's a fact. They do.

Of course, pigeon-lovers like to feed
pigeons. They say the city birds would starve
if they didn't feed them. That's probably true.

One lady in New York used to drive up every
day in her big car and feed buttered toast to
pigeons in the park. They were so tame that they
ate right out of her hand.

So, as you can see, there are two sides to the pigeon question.

One side loves them.

The other side hates them.

The trouble is, there really are too many pigeons in our big cities. If there weren't so many, people would never get so worked up about them one way or the other.

Can you guess how many?

How many pigeons do you think there are in a big city like New York?

A thousand? Ten thousand? A million? Oh, probably even more than that. There's a man at City Hall in New York who knows more about wild pigeons than anyone else. His name is Mr. Dalton and he says New York City has at least three million pigeons.

And there are hundreds of thousands in every big city, not only in the United States, but all over the world.

What Is A Pigeon?

A pigeon is a dove.

A dove is a pigeon.

The bird we call "the white dove of peace"
is a pigeon. And the dove we read about in the
Bible—the one Noah sent from the Ark to find
dry land—that was a pigeon too.

The Arabs have a legend about that. They say
that when the dove returned to the Ark its feet
were covered with pink clay and that's why
pigeons now have pink feet. It isn't true, but
it's a nice story.

There are many kinds of pigeons, as many as 200 different kinds, each with different feathers and different colors. Some are wild and some are tame.

The tame ones are kept as pets, the way we keep a dog or a cat or a hamster. Some of them are trained to be racing pigeons and messenger pigeons. Others are fancy birds which people keep because they think they're pretty. Some are used for scientific experiments. And many are used for food, the same as chickens.

But the pigeons we see on the streets are wild pigeons. There are more of these than of all the tame birds put together. They find their own homes and food in the city, though many people help them by giving them food.

Pigeon with a message holder tied to its back. A smaller holder would be tied to its leg.

Columba Livia

Almost all pigeons—both the wild ones and the tame ones—are descended from *Rock Doves* which first lived on the rocky coasts and cliffs in Europe and Asia and Africa. Scientists call them *Columba Livia*.

They all have 20 feathers on each wing and 12 on the tail. The feathers are neatly joined together with tiny hooks. That's why we say things are "dovetailed," if they are perfectly joined.

Most wild pigeons have red eyes and pink feet. All of them make a cooing sound like a soft gurgle. That's how they got their name. The word "pigeon" comes from a Latin word—*pipire*—which means "to make a peeping sound."

Most pigeons—except a few of the fancy birds—are great flyers. They can fly fast for hundreds of miles. Under their strong wing muscles they have ten small pockets of air which act like balloons to help them stay up in the air easily.

Their eyes are made for flying, too. They have an extra pair of thin eyelids which are transparent, like eyeglasses. These inner eyelids protect their eyes from dust and wind and rain while they're flying. They have very sharp eyes that can see things as far away as ten miles.

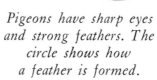

Pigeons have sharp eyes and strong feathers. The circle shows how a feather is formed.

Long ago, in France, an artist drew this picture of pigeons carrying messages.

They can hear just as well as they can see, even though their ears are hidden under the feathers on the sides of their heads.

They also can fly in very cold weather because the temperature of their bodies is 107.2°—much hotter than ours.

But the most interesting thing about pigeons is that they can find their way back to the place they started from, even though it may be hundreds of miles away. No one knows exactly why they can do this, but it gave men like Noah the idea of training them to carry messages. More about that later.

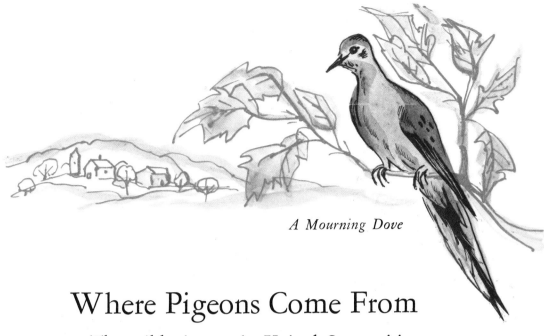

A Mourning Dove

Where Pigeons Come From

The wild pigeons in United States cities are all descended from birds brought here in ships by the early settlers from Europe. They were kept in pigeon coops on the ships and were used for food during the long trip. When the settlers landed, some of the birds left the coops and became wild.

There were millions of wild pigeons in America before the settlers came. They were called Passenger Pigeons but they all died or were cruelly killed off. Wild Mourning Doves probably lived here too, and are still here, but only outside the city, near the woods.

A bird market in ancient China.

In those days farmers kept pigeons the way
farmers keep chickens today. They raised them
for food and for their eggs.

Pigeons have been raised in all countries,
all over the world, since ancient times. The
Egyptians and the Chinese raised pigeons 5,000
years ago. In China, pigeons were favorite
pets. People used to tie bells or bamboo
whistles around the pigeons' necks so the
birds would make music while they were flying.

For more than 2,000 years, pigeons have been trained to carry messages. It was done this way: A bird was taken far away from its home. Then a message was tied to its ankle or its back and the bird would fly straight home with the message. That's why they were called "homing" pigeons.

The ancient Greeks used pigeons to carry news of the winners in their Olympic games. Ancient Romans also used them to send messages home from their armies far away. And the Sultan of Bagdad started a fast pigeon post service to all parts of his empire in the year 1146.

Mail for the Sultan.

Messenger pigeon of World War II
flying with a tiny automatic camera
strapped in front of its breast.

The biggest use of messenger pigeons has
always been in wartime. During World War I
(1914–1918) the Allied armies kept 300,000
pigeons to carry messages. In World War II
(1939–1945) the U. S. Army had more than
3,000 men training pigeons to be messengers.
Some of the birds even had tiny automatic
cameras tied to their breasts and were sent
out to take pictures of enemy positions. Many
of the birds became heroes and were given
medals for their work.

A prize-winning Racing Homer.

We don't need messenger pigeons now because we have radio and telephone, but many people still keep racing pigeons. In Belgium, today, pigeon racing is a national sport, even more popular than horse racing in the United States. These birds are called Racing Homers. They can fly 70 miles an hour and 600 miles in one day. Some Homers fly farther than that. There's a story about one pigeon that was born in China and then was taken to France by plane. It flew back to China in three weeks and that was 7,200 miles.

Racing Homers are not the only pigeons kept as pets. There are many kinds of fancy pigeons that people keep because they like the way they look. Some of them can hardly fly at all and some of them do tricks.

White Fantail

Jacobin

Swallow

Pouter

Tumblers

There's another kind of tame pigeon that isn't a pet and isn't trained to do anything. It's raised for food, on a pigeon farm, the way we raise chickens or turkeys.

Pigeon eggs and pigeon pie were very popular in England a long time ago. You can still see how the pigeons were raised in those days. On an ancient farm in England there is a pigeon house which was built more than 600 years ago. It's called a *dovecote*. It's made of stone and it looks like a round fortress with a pointed roof. Inside, there's a big room about 20 feet wide and 30 feet high, with a hole in the roof through which the birds flew in and out. The walls of the room are full of little caves, each cave just big enough for a pigeon family. That's where they lived and laid their eggs.

Pigeon pie for supper.

*An ancient stone pigeon house
like this one still stands
in Minster Lovell, England.*

Even though there are so many different kinds
of tame pigeons, many more pigeons in the world
today are *not* trained and are *not* raised for
food. These are the wild birds we see on city
streets. There are more of them now than ever.

33

Why Pigeons Live in Cities

Pigeons live in cities because the old buildings in a city are very much like the rocky sea cliffs which were their natural homes. Old city buildings are full of ledges, nooks, crannies, corners, and statues which make good nesting places. That's where the pigeons sleep and build their nests.

The new skyscrapers don't have good nesting places and if all the old buildings were torn down we would probably lose most of the pigeons. But, for the time being, pigeons find many places to build their nests in our cities.

They live on window ledges, on sheltered places under rooftops, especially in the nooks and crannies of old churches, fire houses, libraries, and old armory buildings. You sometimes see them under air conditioners on window ledges. Often, pigeons take over empty buildings.

They like to stand on flat places, so you
won't see them roosting on telephone wires.
They don't build nests in trees like other
birds. That's why it's hard to see pigeon
nests in the city. They're hidden away in
secret places around the buildings, especially
in corners away from the northeast wind. But
if you look for them with binoculars, you'll
be surprised at how many you can find.

Where Pigeons Go in Winter

In winter, many birds go south where it's warm. But not pigeons. Because their blood is hotter than ours, they don't seem to mind the cold, so they can stay in the same place all year round. Also, underneath their outside feathers they have another layer of fine, very soft feathers which is like the warm winter lining in your coat.

Besides that, a fine white powder—called "milt"—covers their outside feathers and keeps them from getting too wet. Pigeons also waterproof their feathers by covering them with oil which they take from under their tail feathers. A pigeon smears some of the oil on its beak and then pulls the feathers through its beak, one at a time. This is known as "preening."

In spite of all this, pigeons have a hard time in winter. There is less food on the streets and not much water when everything is frozen or covered with snow. That's why you see them near steam pipes or chimneys where some of the ice and snow has melted.

Most birds drink water by filling their beaks and tipping their heads back, but a pigeon drinks by sucking up the water the way you drink soda with a straw.

In summer, pigeons have a much easier life. The layers of feathers that keep them warm in winter also keep them cool in summer. There's also more food for them on the streets and more water for them to drink, even though sometimes it's only the water dripping from an air conditioner. They need lots of water, and they use some of it to keep their eggs moist. When the eggs are moist it's easier for the baby chicks to break out of their shells.

In summer, there's also more water for bathing, and pigeons love to bathe. In Venice, Italy, we once saw a pigeon standing perfectly still under a street fountain and letting the water drip on its head. It was taking a shower.

How City Pigeons Find Food

A pigeon needs about one pound of food every week.

When you stop to think about that, it's quite remarkable that all those millions of pigeons can find enough food to eat in the city. Their natural food is grass, berries, and seeds. But there isn't much food like that in the city.

So they've changed their diet. They now live on food people give them—dry bread, popcorn, peanuts, crackers, and such things.

They have become good garbage collectors.
They eat just about anything they can find on
the streets. They even eat stones.

They eat gravel, or grit, which is made up
of tiny sharp stones. They have no teeth and
they need the grit to help them grind up their
food. When you see a pigeon pecking at the
ground, and no food is in sight, it's probably
pecking at stones.

But even so, if people didn't feed them,
there would be very few pigeons in the cities.
We know there are millions of them so it's
clear that a great many people like pigeons.

St. Mark's Square, Venice, Italy

People take care of pigeons in cities all over the world. One of the most famous places for pigeon-lovers is St. Mark's Square in Venice where you can buy special pigeon food. A lot of people come there just to feed the pigeons and many of them want to have their pictures taken with the pigeons eating right out of their hands.

Pigeon Families

If you watch pigeons in the city you will often see one pigeon strutting about in front of another pigeon, puffing out its chest. That will be the father pigeon, showing off before the mother pigeon. He often brings her presents of food, and usually the two birds put their beaks together, very much like two people kissing. This means the two pigeons are ready to mate and start a family.

After the parents mate, the mother pigeon builds a nest with twigs, straw, scraps of paper, or other things that the father pigeon brings to her. The nest is usually in some secret place on the outside of a building away from the wind. It may even be under an air conditioner.

Sitting on the eggs.

About a week after mating, the mother pigeon lays one egg in the nest. Then, two days later, she lays another. Both the mother and father birds take turns sitting on the eggs to keep them warm and make them hatch. The father sits during the day, from about 10 A.M. to about 4:30 P.M. The mother sits all the rest of the time. So, if you look at a clock you will know whether it's the mother or the father pigeon sitting on the eggs.

It takes about 18 days for the eggs to hatch. The baby pigeons are called squabs.

When the squabs are hatched they are naked and helpless. They can't see and they can't hold their heads up straight. The mother and the father birds take turns feeding them.

A squab, just hatched.

The way they do this is very unusual because pigeons are the only birds who feed their babies in this way. What they do is make a soft, creamy food inside their own bodies. It's called "pigeon milk" and they pump it into the mouths of the baby pigeons. Both the mother and father birds make pigeon milk.

This goes on for about a week. Then the parents stop making pigeon milk and give their squabs the same food they eat themselves. First they put the food in their own mouths to make it soft. Then they stuff it into the squab's mouth. It's hard work for the mother and father pigeon because the squabs are hungry all the time.

But they grow fast. In about 3 weeks the squabs have grown feathers and they begin to explore outside the nest. By the time they are 4 or 5 weeks old they are full grown and they fly away. In another week or so they are ready to have squabs of their own.

Squabs, 3 weeks old.

We hardly ever see baby pigeons on the street because they stay in their nests until they are almost full grown. But sometimes you can hear them squeaking.

When pigeons mate and have squabs, the parents usually live together the rest of their lives, having as many as 12 squabs every year.

And That's the Problem!

Every mother pigeon lays from 12 to 14 eggs each year and a pigeon often lives to be 15 years old.

So you can see that if every egg turned into a pigeon and if they all stayed alive for 15 years, very soon there would be many more pigeons than people in the world.

But not all the pigeon eggs hatch. Also, many of the eggs are eaten by rats. And many of the pigeons who *do* grow up are killed by cats, rats, mice, owls, and hawks. Even in big cities there still are hawks who swoop down on the pigeons and carry them away.

In spite of this, the pigeon population keeps on growing in the cities and people have been trying for years to get rid of them in a hundred different ways.

Here are some of the many things people have tried in cities all over the world:

Shooting — In Buffalo, N.Y. they put 7 men on the job. From 8 to 9:30 every morning, these men went out with rifles and shot pigeons. What an ugly way to make a living! And it did not help much. There are still lots of pigeons in Buffalo.

Poisoning — In Boston, Mass. they put out poisoned corn feed. Some of the pigeons died, but there were lots more where those came from, so the poisoning didn't help much in the long run.

Scaring — People have tried to scare pigeons away with firecrackers, noisemakers, and fake owls. It's a waste of money. The pigeons just go to other buildings and come back later.

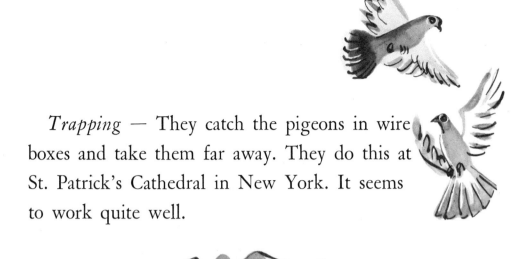

Trapping — They catch the pigeons in wire boxes and take them far away. They do this at St. Patrick's Cathedral in New York. It seems to work quite well.

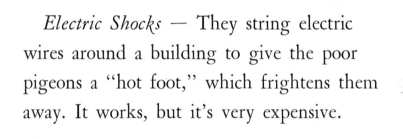

Electric Shocks — They string electric wires around a building to give the poor pigeons a "hot foot," which frightens them away. It works, but it's very expensive.

Spikes — They put metal spikes on the ledges of a building. It doesn't seem to work at all, because the pigeons use the spikes to hold their nests in place.

Jelly — They cover the ledges of a building with sticky jelly which the pigeons hate. It *does* keep them away, but it's hard to tell which is worse—the mess the jelly makes, or the mess the pigeons make.

Sloping Ledges — They fix all the buildings and give them sloping ledges. Pigeons want flat places and won't roost on a sloping ledge. It seems like a great deal of trouble and expense just to keep the pigeons away.

Drugs — They give the pigeons drugged food which knocks them out for a while. Then they pick them up and take them out to the country.

Screening — They put up wire screening on all the places a pigeon might decide to roost. It's almost as expensive as electric wires, and it looks ugly.

Egg Control — This is a sensible idea. It was tried in New York and it seems to work. They put into the pigeon food a special chemical which keeps the eggs from hatching.

So, as you can see, people have gone to a lot of trouble to get rid of pigeons.

A good plan is the one used by the people of a city called Karlsruhe in Germany. They didn't try to get rid of *all* the pigeons. They just found a way to keep down the *number* of pigeons in their city.

They did this by building pigeon coops in the city parks. The coops are comfortable pigeon hotels and the pigeons don't have to search for their food. So most of the Karlsruhe pigeons have come to live in the park houses.

The pigeon coops are on stilts and have removable sides. When the pigeons lay their eggs, a caretaker climbs up, takes down the sides, and pricks the eggs with a needle. Then they don't hatch. And Karlsruhe no longer has too many pigeons.

*Plan for the pigeon coops
built in Karlsruhe, Germany.
A pigeon apartment house.*

Many people think the Karlsruhe plan is the most sensible one. They think it's a good plan because:

1. It keeps down the number of pigeons in a city.

2. It keeps the pigeons from messing up the buildings and the statues, since they stay in their coops in the parks.

3. It's cheaper to give the pigeons houses and food than it is to clean up the mess they make with their droppings.

Of course, this plan will only work when there are more parks in all the cities—even little parks for pigeons and for the people who like pigeons.

And that's a very good idea!

When there are pigeons in a city everybody
can have the pleasure of seeing wild birds
flying free. And perhaps one day you will
be lucky. Perhaps, one day, a pair of pigeons
will build a nest near your window so that
you can watch them day by day.

Then you will see the marvelous way the
squabs hatch out of their eggs; and how they
hold open their pink mouths, like trumpets,
while their parents feed them; and how they
grow and grow and grow, day by day, until they
flap their wings and fly away.

Wouldn't that be a wonderful thing to see?

Index